PRAISE My Pet:

ADULT COLORING BOOK

WWW.PRAISEMYPET.COM

Color Xena Warrior Princess!

Color Sir Ron and Simba!

8

Color Velvet, Zelda and Kiki!

9

Color Versace, Chi, Jasmine and Yumi!

14

Color Bentley Boo!

Color Cloudy and Big Ox!

15

Color Lennoxx and Linkin!

Color Ciroq!

17

Color Mary, Jazzie, Bella and Precious Prissy!

18

Color Pongo and Precious!

21

Color Chevy!

Color Pickles and Hunney!

23

Color Milah and Lexie!

25

Color Starky!

Color Rufus and Jabez!

26

Color Murphee and Baylee!

Color Gordy!

27

Color Harley and Wetta!

28

Color Coco, Lulu and Kona!

29

Color Buzz, Midnight and Nena!

32

Color Sweetpea!

Color Buddy and Chance!

33

Color Elaine, Nala and Babygirl!

34

Color Jack!

Color Coco and Cooper!

35

Color Taylor!

Color Rexi and Moki!

36

Color Sissy and Teddy!

Color Reggie Magoo!

37

Color Lucy, Drake, Snoopy and Pharrell!

Color ChiChi!

Color Luna and Putter!

39

Color Mimi!

Color Zowie and Mia!

42

Color Molly, Chase and Charlie!

45

Color Rosie and Henry!

Color Maddy!

47

Color Iszak!

Color Willie and Mazie!

Color Coco Puff!

Color Rocky and Bella!

49

Color Bella!

Color Monster and Sweet Pea!

50

Color Baby, Cleo and Lucky!

51

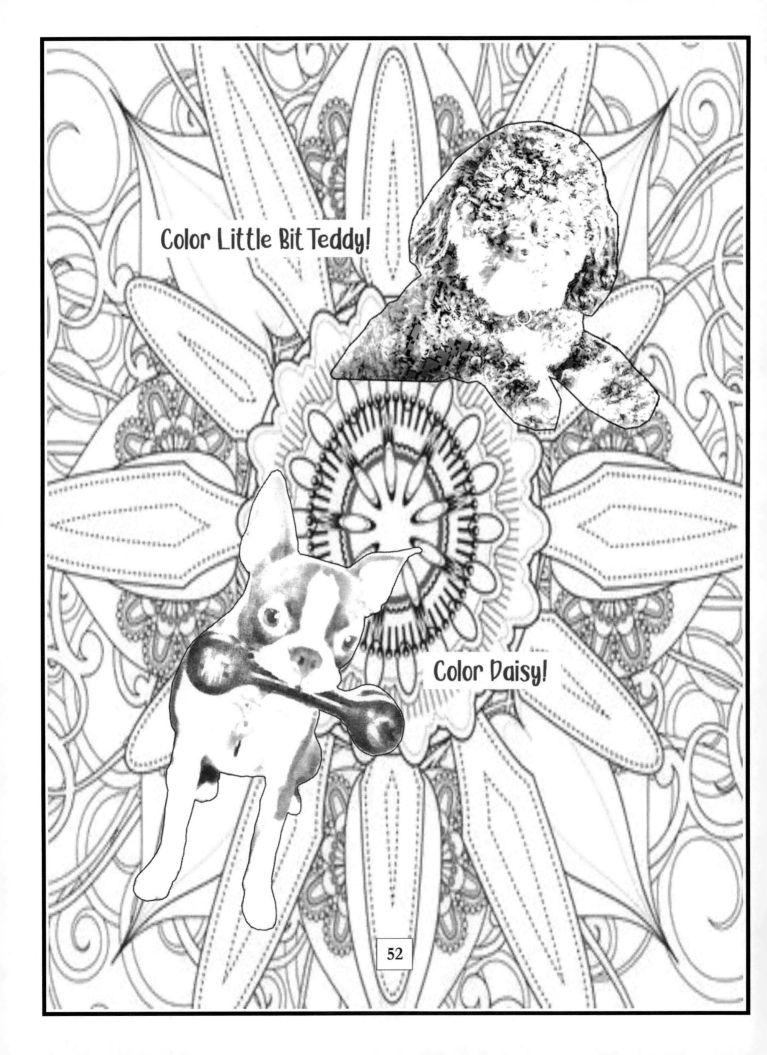

Color Little Bit Teddy!

Color Daisy!

52

Color Itsy and Savvy!

Color Juno!

Color Pooch, Gizmo, Walter and Stimpy!

54

Color Dora, Eddie and Bubby!

56

Color Turbo!

Color Storm, Lorenzo and Mayumi!

58

60

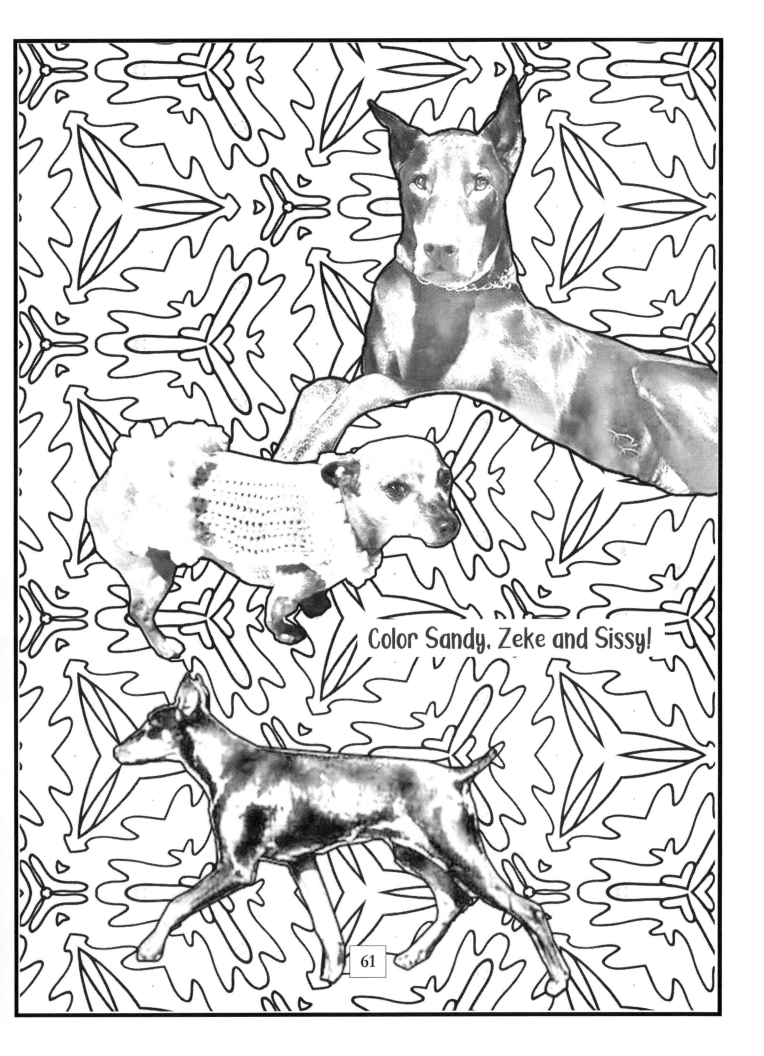

Color Sandy, Zeke and Sissy!

61

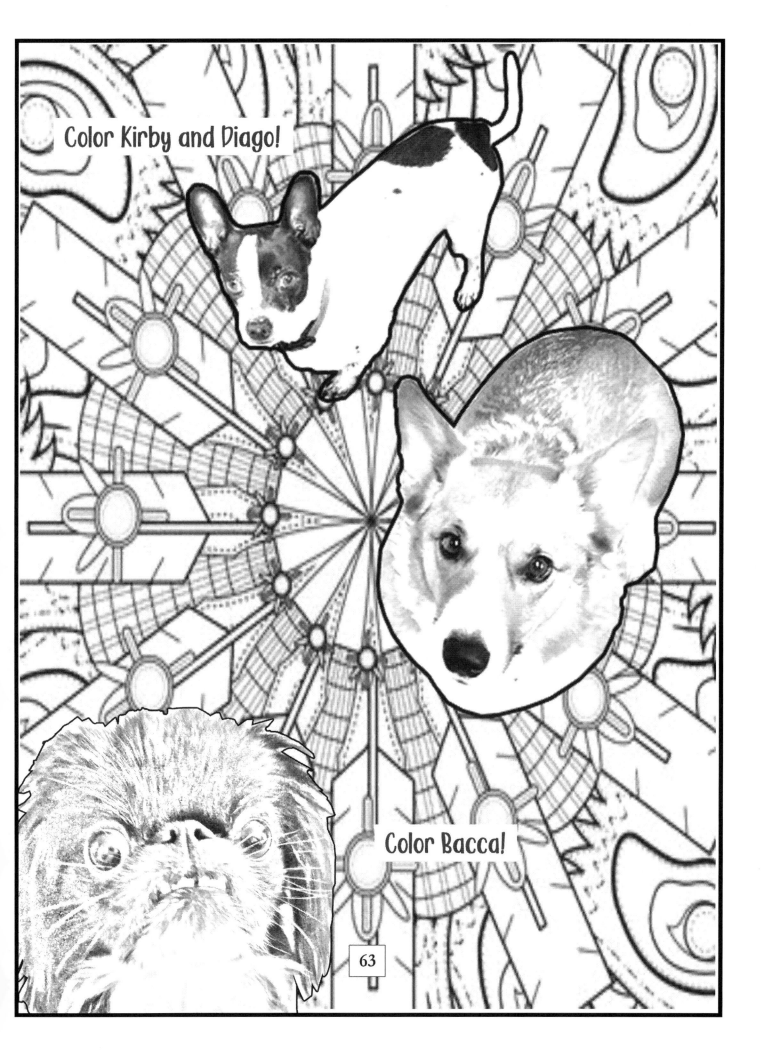

Color Kirby and Diago!

Color Bacca!

63

Color Max!

Color Mollie and Maddie!

64

Color Bella!

Color Louie and Lola!

65

Color Pony Boy, Cherry, Bronx, and Shadow!

68

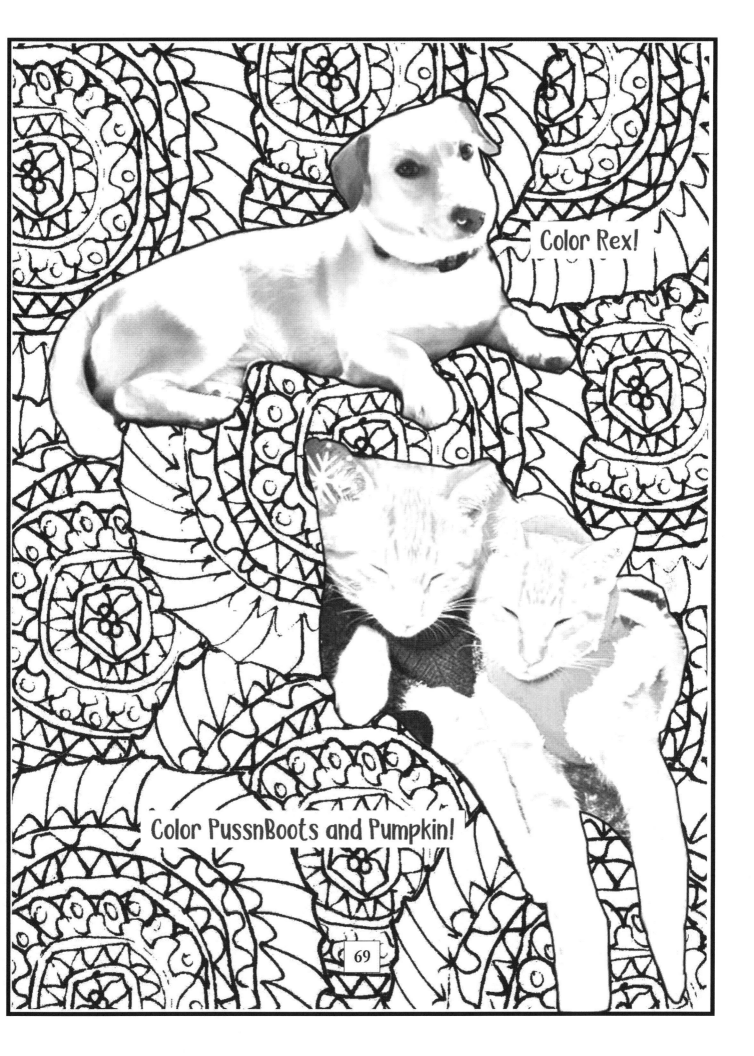

Color Diesel, Chopper and Layla!

70

Color Crackle!

Color Wrigley!

72

Color Sallie Mae!

76

Color Bardi Girl, Lambeau and Reggie!

78

Color Ruggie!

91

Color Brandi!

Color Cash!

Color Darshawn!

93

Color Daisy!

Color Wishbone!

100

Color Ginger!

Color Tikii!

102

We hope you enjoyed our coloring book! If you'd like to see YOUR pet in one of our upcoming coloring books, visit www.praisemypet.com/pages/send-us-your-pet-photos

Happy coloring!

Made in the USA
Columbia, SC
20 February 2021